FRIENDS OF ZION MUSEUM

מוזיאון ידידי ישראל

A Lighthouse of Hope and Love

Friends of Zion Museum: A Lighthouse of Hope and Love

Published by Friends of Zion Heritage Center
20 Yosef Rivlin Street Nahalat Shiv'a' Jerusalem 94240

Designed and produced by dpc&s.
Art direction and design by Dean Wilder.
Interior photographic imaging by Brandon L. Hull and Terry C. Montague of Regal 360

ISBN: 978-1-62961-087-0

FRIENDS OF ZION MUSEUM

מוזיאון ידידי ישראל

A Lighthouse of Hope and Love

Published by Friends of Zion Heritage Center

Also I heard the voice of the Lord, saying: "Whom shall I send, And who will go for Us?" Then I said,

"Here am I! Send me."

—Isaiah 6:8

When Prime Minister Benjamin Netanyahu spoke those words in August 2012, he declared the belief of a number of Jewish leaders. Theodor Herzl, the father of the modern Jewish state, dreamed of the day it might become a reality.

As if to encourage himself and his friends, he wrote: "If you will it, it is no dream." No words could more clearly apply to the Friends of Zion Museum in Jerusalem. For centuries the Biblical prophecies of Jews returning to their homeland seemed like only a distant dream, yet a dream remembered year after year with Jews repeating the promise "next year in Jerusalem."

Supporting this dream for a homeland, throughout history Christian Zionists have stood courageously with and, in many cases, sacrificed their lives protecting the Jewish people.

Although there is an increasing awareness in Israel of the historic support of Christians, many remain unaware of these Christian heroes, such as Corrie ten Boom whose father gave his life to save God's Chosen People, and those who helped establish the present-day state of Israel. The Friends of Zion Museum exists to tell their story.

Sing praises to the Lord, who dwells in Zion! Declare His deeds among the people. – Psalm 9:11

So the Lord gave to Israel all the land of which He had sworn to give to their fathers, and they took possession of it and dwelt in it. – Joshua 21:43

Welcome

A Message from former Israeli Prime Minister
Shimon Peres
International Chairman of the Friends of Zion Museum

Dear Friends,

It is my esteemed pleasure to welcome you to the Friends of Zion Heritage Center. It is my real privilege to welcome you to this unique institution.

It tells the miracle of Israel.

I remember the first day before the state was established as I do remember the preceding history.

We are very grateful to all the people who created this miracle because it was a miracle of people, including friends of Zion, Jewish and not Jewish.

Nothing is greater than the cause of friendship among human beings.

Welcome to the Land of Israel

Then you shall know that I am the Lord, when I bring you into the land of Israel, into the country for which I raised My hand in an oath to give to your fathers. – Ezekiel 20:42

The Red Sea

Negev Desert

Northern Negev

Negev Desert

Jaffa – Tel Aviv

And I have put My words in your mouth; I have covered you with the shadow of My hand, That I may plant the heavens, Lay the foundations of the earth, And say to Zion, "You are My people." – Isaiah 51:16

Jaffa – Tel Aviv

Caesarea

Haifa

Sea of Galilee

Mount Hermon

Galilee

Jordan Valley

Dead Sea

Zin Valley

A Message from
Dr. Michael D. Evans,
Founder of the Friends of Zion Museum

Here am I in the Zin Valley in the heart of Israel's Negev Desert.

Three thousand years ago, the children of Israel passed through this valley on their way from Egypt to Canaan in fulfillment of a Divine promise.

No nation has ever been destroyed again and again and then reborn... but these people accomplished precisely that...and in the same place after two millennia.

Even the skeptics have called it a miracle!

The Friends of Zion Heritage Center pays tribute to their story by celebrating a remarkable group of men and women: non-Jews who helped the people of the Promise to return to the land of their birthright. For them it was a HERE AM I moment

May you be inspired by their story and may you, too, say "Here Am I" (Hineni)

Time Machine Elevator

The story you are about to experience does not begin in 1948 when Israel became a state...nor the two centuries before when it was but a dream of visionaries.

It starts with a promise,
and it begins almost
4,000 years ago...

Time Machine Elevator

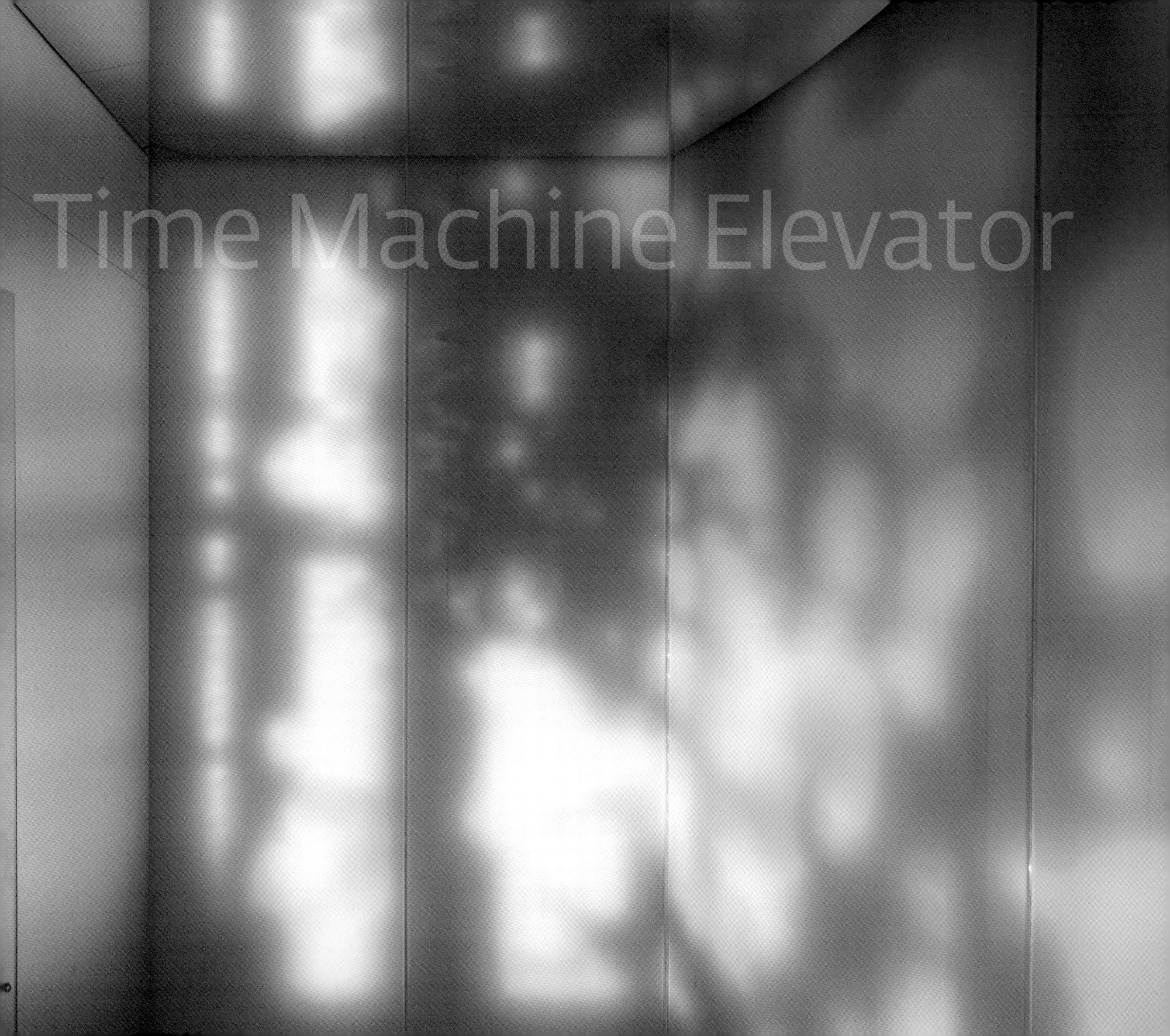

Founders Theater

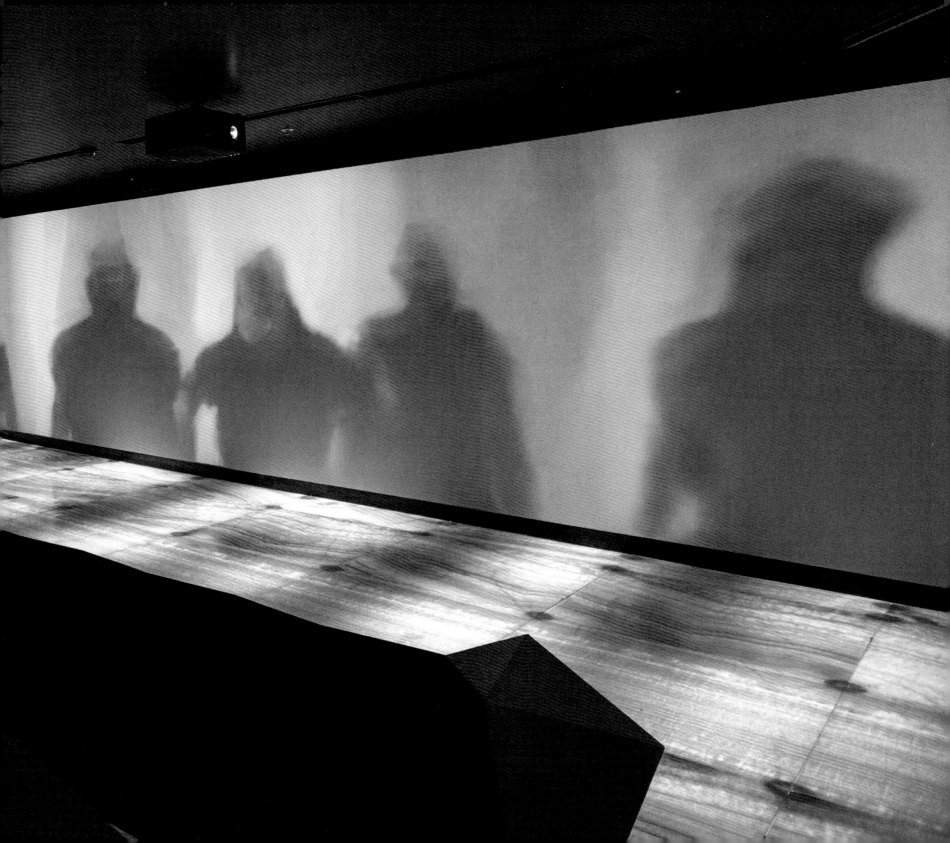

Founders Theater

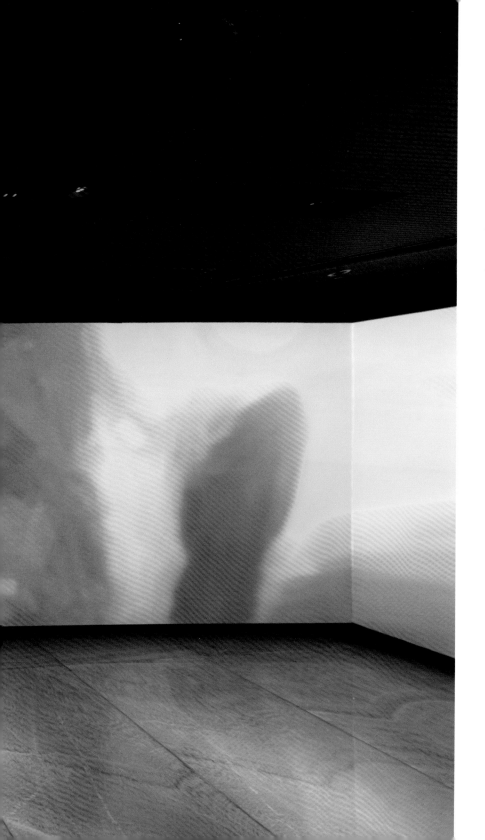

The ancient Hebrew texts say "the eyes of the Lord run to and fro throughout the whole earth, to show Himself strong on behalf of those whose heart is loyal to Him..."

The Lord seemed to have found such a loyal-hearted man in the deserts of Canaan. His name was Abram, son of Terah, from Ur of the Chaldees...

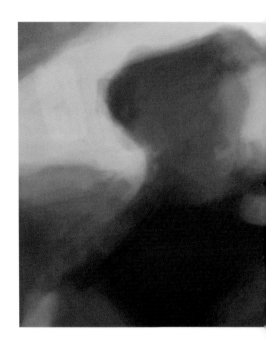

According to the ancient writings...

One day, God appeared to Abram and spoke
the words that would give birth to the nation
of Israel.

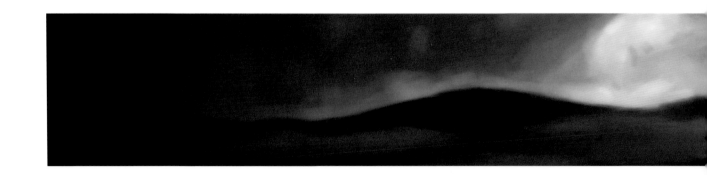

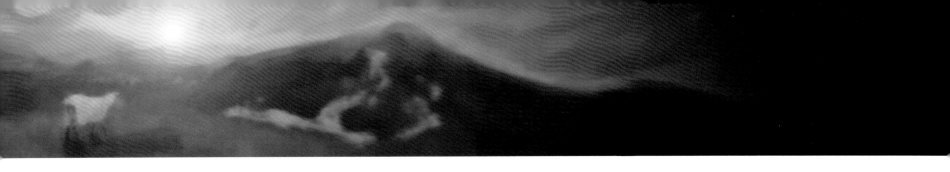

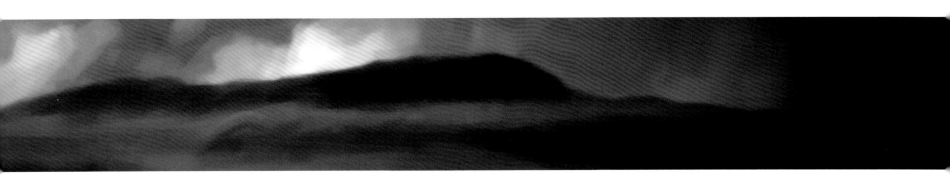

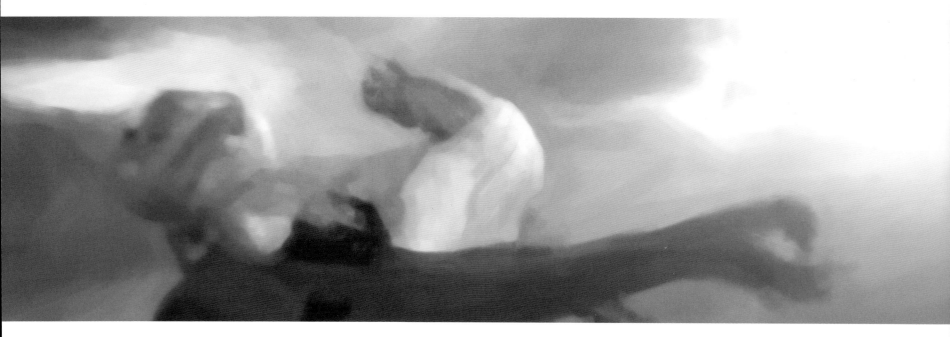

God told Abram, "Get out of your country, from your family, and from your father's house...to a land that I will show you. I will make you a great nation; I will bless you and make your name great...I will establish my covenant as an everlasting covenant between Me and your descendants...to be your God. The whole land of Canaan...I will give as an everlasting possession to you and your descendants."

"I will bless those who bless you and I will curse him who curses you; And in you all the nations of the earth will be blessed."

"...You will no longer be called Abram; your name will be Abraham, for I have made you a father of many nations."

Can you imagine how impossible this promise must have seemed to Abraham?

Founders Theater

Nevertheless, in total faith Abraham said, "Hineni—Here Am I" to the call of God. In obedience to the vision, he and his family began the long journey to Canaan, the land he believed God had said would become his home...

And the generations of Abraham to follow would grow to be a great nation, the children of Israel, the people of the Promise...

Before that promise was realized, Israel would endure 400 years of brutal slavery in Egypt. But in the midst of their suffering, a Hebrew man named Moses, exiled in the mountains of Midian, one day saw a vision of God in a burning bush.

In his own "Hineni—Here Am I" moment, Moses accepted the call to lead his people out of bondage.

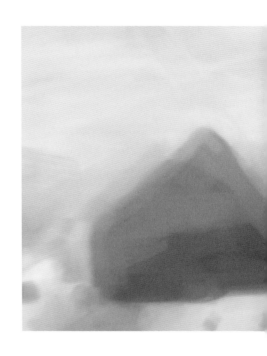

41

Founders Theater

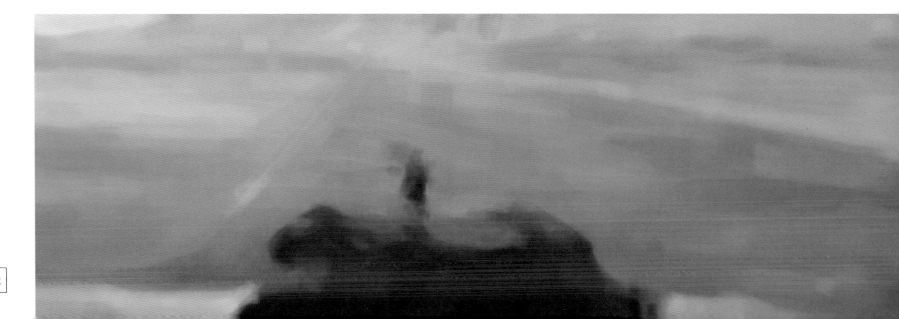

42

Just before Moses died, God took him to a high point overlooking Caanan and showed him the Promised Land.

Though Moses never entered it himself, the children of Israel were about to see the promise to Abraham fulfilled…

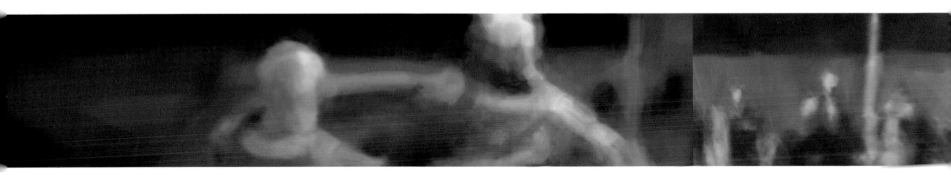

Battles would be fought. Miracles would be recorded. Victories would be celebrated. Ultimately, Israel would occupy the land just as it had been promised...

It was Israel's Golden Age. It would not last...

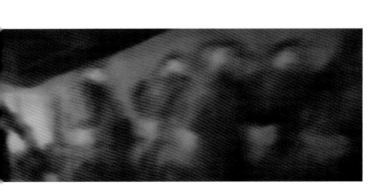

Founders Theater

Not every generation would serve or even believe the covenant of the Promise.

In 70 A.D. Roman legions marched on Jerusalem. The city was sacked. The Great Temple burned to the ground. A million Jews were slaughtered. Most of the rest were marched away into captivity. The Kingdom of Israel was no more.

The promise SEEMED to be over...but was it?

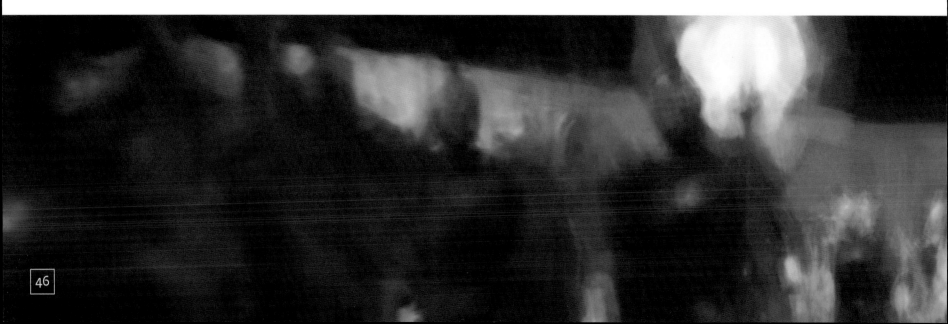

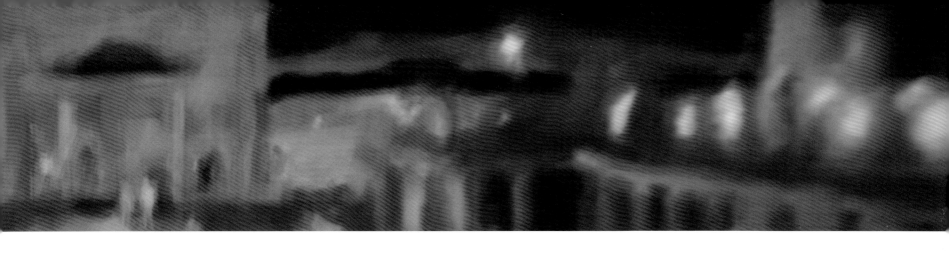

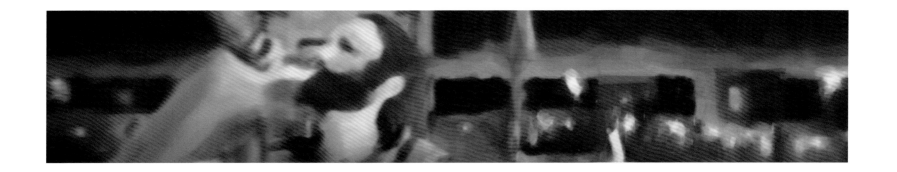

Founders Theater

A thousand years before, the prophet EZEKIEL was at prayer one day…

Ezekiel found himself standing before a valley filled with dry bones…human bones…

As the prophet gazed upon the scene, God asked him if these bones could live, to which Ezekiel wisely replied, "O Lord God, YOU know!"

What happened then must have been quite a sight to behold…

Founders Theater

God told Ezekiel to speak to the bones and command them to live. The prophet later wrote:

So I prophesied as I was commanded. And as I was prophesying, there was a noise, a rattling sound, and the bones came together, bone to bone. I looked and tendons and flesh appeared on them and skin covered them...Then He said to me, "...These are the people of Israel...My people. I am going to open your graves and bring you up from them; I will bring you back to the land of Israel."

God told Ezekiel this was the House of Israel.
Just as these dry, dead bones had been restored
to life, so Israel would be restored.

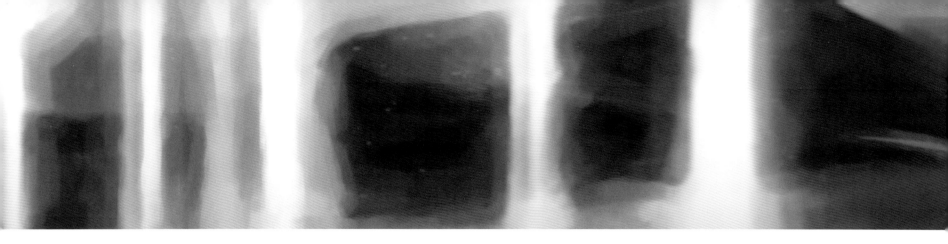

As the nation of Israel settled in exile among the nations, the prayer continued year after year around the world:

"Next year in Jerusalem..."

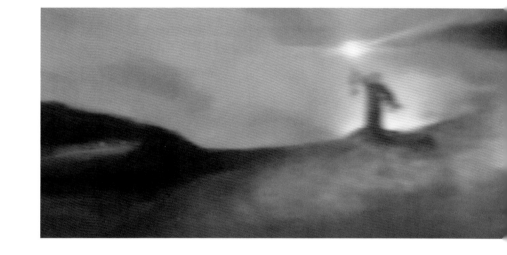

Founders Theater

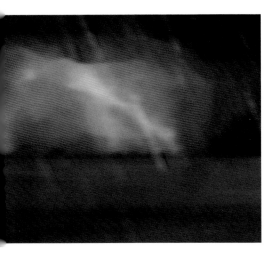

As the years became decades, then centuries, for many, the promise seemed little more than a distant dream of the past.

Most of the Jews resigned themselves to building new lives among the nations where they had gone.

More often, they encountered rejection, persecution, even faced death at the hands of those who did not believe the promise... and if they did, had no intention of letting it be fulfilled.

Yet the Jews found others who also believed the ancient prophecies and who offered their help to see them fulfilled. In their own way, like the patriarchs of old, when their time came, they, too, would say,

"Here Am I"...to the Promise and the People of the Land of Israel.

They would be called Christian Zionists.

The Dreamers

"I will bring them out from the nations and gather them from the countries, and I will bring them into their own land."

Ezekiel 34:13

"I will bring back my exiled people Israel. They will rebuild the ruined cities and live in them. They will plant vineyards and drink their wine. They will make gardens and eat their fruit. I will plant Israel in their own land, never again to be uprooted from the land I have given them."

Amos 9:14-15

The Dreamers

"I will bring you from the nations and gather you from the countries where you have been scattered – with a mighty hand and an outstretched arm and with outpoured wrath."

Ezekiel 20:34

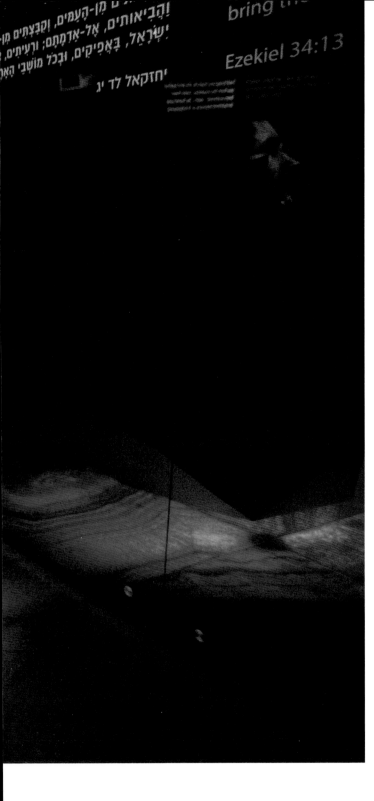

By the 19th century, Christian dreamers were beginning to publicly voice their belief in the Promise.

Here are four who represent these dreamers…

Early 19th-century Believers who raised their voices in support of the Jewish return to the land of Israel.

The Dreamers

Willem and Elisabeth ten Boom

Willem and Elisabeth ten Boom were devout Dutch Christians.

The ten Booms opened a clock shop in Haarlem, just outside Amsterdam, in 1837 and lived with their family in the small apartment above the shop.

Their apartment became the setting for one of the most powerful events in history. That is, if you believe in the power of prayer.

Believing the ancient prophecies of the Bible and moved by the injunction of Psalm 122:6 that reads, "Pray for the Peace of Jerusalem, May those who love you be secure," in 1844, the ten Booms opened their humble home every week to lead a group of Christians in prayer for the Holy City, its inhabitants, and for the Jews then scattered around the world.

Their son Casper and his young wife Cornelia continued the tradition, joined by their children, Betsie, Corrie, Nollie, and Willem.

By then, the ten Boom Prayer Meeting was an established part of the Christian community life in Haarlem.

The last weekly ten Boom Jerusalem prayer meeting took place on February 28, 1944, 100 years to the day when Willem and Elisabeth had started them.

The ten Booms don't show up in many history books of the 20th century. But in those 100 years of faithful weekly gatherings, the ten Booms led over 5,200 intercessory prayer meetings on behalf of the city of Jerusalem and the people of the Promise.

In 1988, Dr. Michael Evans restored the ten Boom house in Haarlem and opened it as a museum, a forerunner and the inspiration for the Friends of Zion Museum in Jerusalem.

William Blackstone

Born in 1841, William Blackstone was a devout Christian.
One night, young William experienced an all-night soul-searching. The next morning, he renounced all material pursuit and devoted his life to advancing his faith. Soon afterward, his study of prophetic Scriptures led him to a deep conviction of the Jewish people's Divinely ordained right to their biblical homeland.

In 1878, he authored a bestselling book that sold millions of copies worldwide. In it, he spoke of Israel's survival in exile…

"Their wonderful preservation as a distinct people…is a standing miracle, attesting the truth of God's Word, and assuring us of His purposes in their future history…I could fill a book with comments about how Israel WILL be restored, but all I have desired to do [is] to show that it is an INCONTROVERTIBLE fact of history."

In 1891, he crafted a petition to be privately presented to the world's leaders. It called for support of a Jewish homeland in ancient Palestine. The petition was signed by 413 prominent leaders. It came to be called "The Blackstone Memorial" and gave a powerful voice to the Zionist cause.

He wrote: "Why shall not the powers which gave Bulgaria to the Bulgarians and Serbia to the Serbians, now give Palestine back to the Jews? These provinces…were wrested from the Turks and given to their natural owners. Does not Palestine as rightfully belong to the Jews?"

When Theodor Herzl and other Jewish Zionist leaders were considering an offer from the British government to establish a Jewish homeland in Uganda, Blackstone marked up his personal Bible with all of the prophetic passages underlined which called for the return of the Children of Israel to the Promised Land. He sent the Bible to Herzl, who is said to have kept it on his desk for most of his life.

William Blackstone died in 1935, 13 years before his dream would come true.

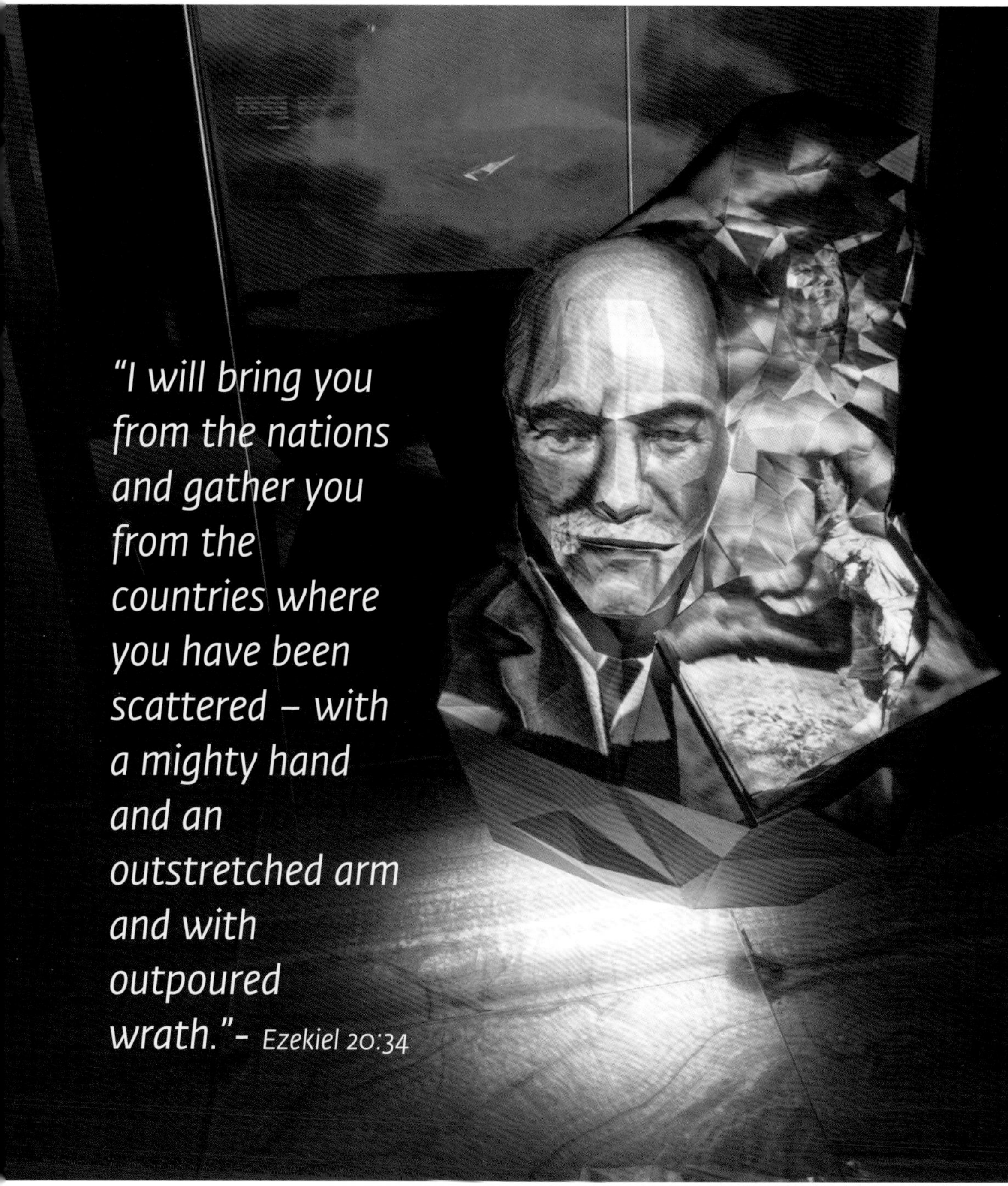

"I will bring you from the nations and gather you from the countries where you have been scattered – with a mighty hand and an outstretched arm and with outpoured wrath." – *Ezekiel 20:34*

וְהוֹצֵאתִי אֶתְכֶם,
מִן-הָעַמִּים, וְקִבַּצְתִּי
אֶתְכֶם, מִן-הָאֲרָצוֹת
אֲשֶׁר נְפוֹצֹתֶם
בָּם--בְּיָד חֲזָקָה
וּבִזְרוֹעַ נְטוּיָה, וּבְחֵמָה
שְׁפוּכָה.

- יחזקאל כ לד

61

The Dreamers

you from the nations, and gather
the countries where you have
dered – with a mighty hand and
tched arm and with outpoured

el 20:34

"וְהוֹצֵאתִים מִן-הָעַמִּים, וְקִבַּצְתִּים מִן-הָאֲרָצוֹת,
וַהֲבִיאוֹתִים, אֶל-אַדְמָתָם; וּרְעִיתִים, אֶל-הָרֵי
יִשְׂרָאֵל, בָּאֲפִיקִים, וּבְכֹל מוֹשְׁבֵי הָאָרֶץ."

יחזקאל לד יג

"I will bring them
out from the
nations and
gather them from
the countries, and
I will bring them
into their own
land." – *Ezekiel 34:13*

וְהוֹצֵאתִים מִן-הָעַמִּים,
וְקִבַּצְתִּים
מִן-הָאֲרָצוֹת,
וַהֲבִיאוֹתִים,
אֶל-אַדְמָתָם;
וּרְעִיתִים, אֶל-הָרֵי
יִשְׂרָאֵל, בָּאֲפִיקִים,
וּבְכֹל מוֹשְׁבֵי הָאָרֶץ.

- יחזקאל לד יג

John Henry Dunant

Few men in modern history have done more to promote care for the suffering than John Henry Dunant, a Swiss born businessman, humanitarian, and a devout Christian.

As a young man of 24, he helped found the Geneva chapter of the YMCA and became a driving force behind the international YMCA movement.

In Italy, he witnessed firsthand the horrors of war. Appalled at the indifference of those in power, Dunant organized local citizens to aid suffering and dying men. Thousands were saved. He returned home and led a campaign that resulted in the creation of the International Red Cross to serve without prejudice the wounded of all sides in any war.

A year later, Dunant helped sponsor the Geneva Convention that established humanitarian rules of conduct for war still followed today.

Dunant campaigned vigorously for the establishment of a Jewish homeland. In 1867, he founded the Association For The Resettlement of Palestine.

He said...

"...the moment could not be better for commencing the resettlement of Palestine."

Theodor Herzl, the founder of the Zionist movement, is said to have first coined the phrase "Christian Zionist" in reference to his friend, John

Henry Dunant, one of only a handful of non-Jews invited to the First Zionist Congress in Basel, Switzerland. Dunant died in poverty but not without honor.

In 1901, he was awarded the first Nobel Prize for Peace.

Professor George Bush

Professor George Bush began his career as an ordained Presbyterian minister; however, his influence was not to be from the pulpit but with his pen.

As Professor of Hebrew and Oriental Literature at New York University, the more he studied the ancient languages of the Bible, the more he became convinced of the Biblical prophecies of a Jewish return to their land. He became a national voice calling for the restoration of the Jewish people to their historic homeland.

In 1844, he published his views in a landmark book titled *The Valley of Vision; or, The Dry Bones of Israel Revived* based on the prophecies of Ezekiel in the Bible.

Professor Bush wrote…

"The dispersed and downcast remnant shall, one after another, turn their faces to Zion, and in sparse and scattered bands find their way to the land of their fathers…This will not only benefit the Jews, but all mankind, forming a link of communication between humanity and God… It will flash a splendid demonstration upon all kindreds and tongues."

The Valley of Vision sold more than a million copies, which was unheard of in the era before the Civil War.

His writings had a profound impact in shaping the view of the Jews and their homeland.

Professor George Bush and other courageous voices set the stage for America, a century later, to be the first country to embrace the reborn State of Israel and to remain its strongest friend in the decades since. Two of his distant relations would someday be President of the United States, both deeply committed to a strong Israel in the family of nations.

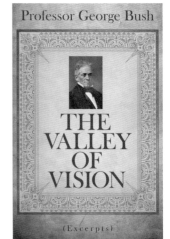

The Dreamers

"I will bring back my exiled people Israel; They will rebuild the ruined cities and live in them. They will plant vineyards and drink their wine; They will make gardens and eat their fruit. I will plant Israel in their own land, never again to be uprooted from the land I have given them."

– Amos 9:14-15

וְשַׁבְתִּי, אֶת-שְׁבוּת
עַמִּי יִשְׂרָאֵל, וּבָנוּ
עָרִים נְשַׁמּוֹת וְיָשָׁבוּ,
וְנָטְעוּ כְרָמִים וְשָׁתוּ
אֶת-יֵינָם; וְעָשׂוּ גַנּוֹת,
וְאָכְלוּ אֶת-פְּרִיהֶם.
וּנְטַעְתִּים,
עַל-אַדְמָתָם; וְלֹא
יִנָּתְשׁוּ עוֹד, מֵעַל
אַדְמָתָם אֲשֶׁר נָתַתִּי
לָהֶם--אָמַר, יְהוָה
אֱלֹהֶיךָ - עמוס ט יד-טו

The Visionaries

Here's to the Visionaries—Late 19th and pre-1948 20th-century Christians who helped bring out the

fulfillment of the
Biblical Promise...

The Visionaries

For Zion's sake I will not hold My peace, And for Jerusalem's sake I will not rest, Until her righteousness goes forth as brightness, And her salvation as a lamp that burns. – Isaiah 62:1

The Visionaries Gallery features leaders who promoted and supported a return of the Jewish people to their ancient homeland.

Dr. Mike D. Evans accompanies former Israeli Prime Minister and Friends of Zion Museum International Chairman Shimon Peres on a tour of the Visionaries Gallery.

1 Edward Robinson

Apr. 10, 1794 – Jan. 27, 1863
United States

The Father of Biblical Geography.

Professor Edward Robinson produced more than 300 significant archeological discoveries in the Holy Land. Among them was King Hezekiah's secret tunnel at the base of a giant arch that once supported a grand staircase to Solomon's Temple, known today as "Robinson's Arch."

This Christian visionary awakened a global awareness and interest in the land of the Bible that set the stage for the rise of the Zionist movement. It would flourish in the decades ahead and call home the People of the Promise.

2 Josiah Wedgwood IV

1st Baron Wedgwood
Mar. 16, 1872 – Jul. 26, 1943
England

Descendant of the famous Wedgwood Pottery family, Josiah Wedgwood IV was an outspoken advocate in Parliament for the Jewish cause in Palestine. He opposed the British reversal of its earlier support of founding a Jewish state in its Biblical homeland and argued against the 1939 White Paper, which strictly limited Jewish immigration to the Holy Land.

He supported Ze'ev Jabotisnki proclaiming that "Ultimately Jews will have to fight for their land, and they should arm and train for that inevitability."

3 Laurence Oliphant

Aug. 3, 1829 – Dec. 23, 1888

Alice Oliphant

Unknown – Jan. 2, 1886
England

In 1880, Laurence wrote *The Land of Gilead* outlining a detailed plan for Jewish resettlement of Palestine under Turkish sovereignty and British protection. The plan failed, and he saw little fruit from his efforts in his lifetime.

Laurence Oliphant's secretary, Naftali Herz Imber was a Jewish Romanian poet who published a collection of his poems (including "Our Hope").

He dedicated the book to his friends, Laurence and Alice Oliphant. Set to music by Samuel Cohen, "Our Hope" became the national anthem of the new state of Israel.

4 Queen Victoria

May 24, 1819 – Jan. 22, 1901
Great Britain

In 1865, Queen Victoria founded and became the patron of the Palestine Exploration Fund, the first organization created to specifically study the history, land, and people of Palestine. This fund produced a body of scientific work that is still serving scholars today.

Taking the land that had been known in Europe only from the Bible, the organization brought it into the real world of the day. Queen Victoria's patronage contributed to a modern recognition of Palestine as the Biblical homeland of the Jews.

5 Woodrow Wilson

Dec. 28, 1856 – Feb. 3, 1924
United States

The son and grandson of Presbyterian ministers, Woodrow Wilson felt destined to be president and someday help restore the Jewish people to their homeland.

As president he nominated Louis Brandeis, a Jew and his close friend, to the Supreme Court. Wilson's support of the Balfour Declaration, announcing the British government's support of a future Jewish state in the land of its history, set the stage for statehood some 30 years later.

6 Winston Churchill

Nov. 30, 1874 – Jan. 24, 1965
Great Britain

Winston Churchill was impressed with the success of the Jewish settlers and disturbed by the Arab hostility to Zionism:

"It is manifestly right that the scattered Jews should have a national center and a national home and be reunited – and where else but in Palestine with which for 3,000 years they have been intimately and profoundly associated?"

Churchill told Chaim Weizmann he believed the Jewish state should

include ALL of Western Palestine and proposed his own Jewish-Arab partition plan of Palestine.

7 Arthur James Balfour
Jul. 25, 1848 – Mar. 19, 1930

David Lloyd George
Jan. 17, 1863 – Mar. 26, 1945
Great Britain

Arthur James Balfour, British Foreign Secretary (formerly Prime Minister from 1902-05), and David Lloyd George, Prime Minister of Great Britain during World War I.

Through their evangelical upbringing, they shared a common faith in the Divine destiny of Israel to be restored to the land of their ancestors.

In 1917, these two courageous men joined with Chaim Weizmann, the new Jewish leader of the Zionist cause, to craft The Balfour Declaration for the British government, announcing Britain's official support of the Zionist vision.

8 Anthony Ashley Cooper
7th Earl of Shaftesbury

Apr. 28, 1801 – Oct. 1, 1885
England

Sir Anthony Cooper promoted the Jewish return to their Palestinian homeland despite popular opinion. He convinced the sultan of Turkey that Jews in Palestine would economically benefit the Ottoman Empire and persuaded His Majesty's government to establish a consulate in Jerusalem.

This devout Christian single-handedly changed British perceptions of the Middle East for the next generation— to support the World Zionist movement and its aims toward a return of the Jews to their ancient homeland.

He did more than anyone before him to translate Christian Zionist themes into a political initiative and set the stage for the rise of the World Zionist movement.

9 Horatio Spafford
Oct. 20, 1828 – Oct. 16, 1888

Anna Spafford
Mar. 16, 1842 – Apr. 17, 1923
United States

The Spaffords lost their home in the Chicago Fire of 1871. Two years later, Anna and their four daughters sailed to England. The ship sank, and all four daughters were drowned at sea. Anna cabled her husband, "Saved alone. What shall I do?"

In his despair, he wrote the now famous hymn, "It Is Well With My Soul."

The Spaffords devoted the rest of their lives to helping the poor and disadvantaged of Jerusalem.

10 Rev. William Henry Hechler
Jan. 10, 1845 – Jan. 31, 1931
Germany / England

Appalled by the brutal anti-Semitic pogroms on Russian Jews, in 1882 William Hechler gathered a group of Russian Christians to help them escape to Palestine.

He said, "It is the duty of every Christian to love the Jew... The return of the Jews would become a blessing to Europe and put an end to the anti-Semitic spirit of hatred, which is most detrimental to the welfare of all nations."

He used his influence to help legitimize the Zionist cause and Theodor Herzl, though many Jewish leaders still rejected his vision of Zionism.

11 Walter Clay Lowdermilk
Jul. 1, 1888 – May 6, 1974
United States

A world-renowned American expert on soil conservation, Walter Lowdermilk was sent to Palestine to report on Jewish settlements. In his book *Palestine, Land of Promise* he wrote:

"I have watched with genuine admiration the steady and unmistakable progress made in the rehabilitation of Palestine which, desolate for centuries, is now renewing its youth and vitality through the enthusiasm, hard work, and self-sacrifice of the Jewish pioneers who toil there in the spirit of peace and social justice.... This cause merits sympathy and moral encouragement of everyone."

Lights in the Darkness

If you extend your soul to the hungry And satisfy the afflicted soul, Then your light shall dawn in the darkness, And your darkness shall be as the noonday.

– Isaiah 58:10

Lights in the Darkness

In the 1930s, Adolf Hitler set in motion his plan to conquer the world and ultimately...to annihilate its Jews.

Tragically, much of the Christian religion in Europe fell prey to an insidious theology that dismissed the suffering of the Jews. And yet there were Christians who knew differently. Some of these Christians risked their own lives to save Jewish lives and become beacons of hope...Lights in the Darkness...

Not all of them were Zionists, but without their courage, there would have been no one left to build a nation when the time did come...

Oskar Schindler

Oskar Schindler just wanted to make money with cheap Jewish labor.

But he began to see his factory as a sanctuary for his Jews.

Saving his Jews from the death trains became his obsession, but it cost him all of his fortune.

Somebody once asked him why he did it. He said,

"I felt the Jews were being destroyed. I had to help them. There was no choice." However, there WAS a choice, and Oskar Schindler made that choice: to save over 1,200 men, women, and children from the Nazi ovens.

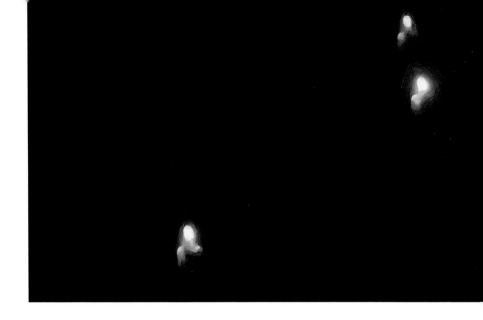

Lights in the Darkness

Irena Sendler

Irena Sendler was a young Catholic nurse in Warsaw, Poland.

When she found out 5,000 Jews were dying every day of starvation and disease behind the walls of the Jewish Ghetto, she determined to do something to help. With forged identification papers, she talked her way past the guards and into the crowded ghetto.

Irena went to the mothers. She told them if their children stayed where they were, they WOULD die. With gut-wrenching pain, these mothers of Israel said goodbye to their boys and girls and babes in arms...

knowing in their hearts they would probably never see them again. And most of them never did.

Irena used carts, coffins, the false bottom of a tool box, and the back of an ambulance to smuggle the children to safety. She placed them in Christian homes, in churches, convents, and Catholic orphanages— wherever they would be safe until after the war.

Irena Sendler had rescued over 2,500 children from the jaws of death.

She said, "Every child saved with my help is the justification of my existence on this earth... not a title to glory."

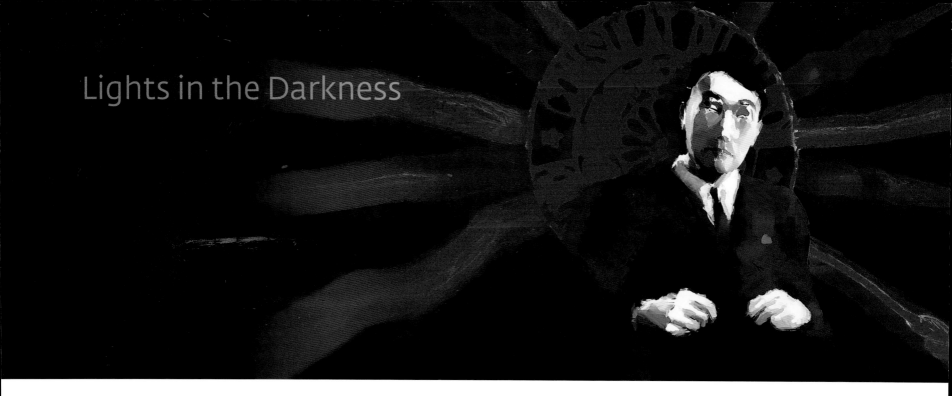

Lights in the Darkness

Chiune Sugihara

As Hitler's war machine swallowed up Europe, thousands of Jews fled East. In Lithuania, hundreds surrounded the Japanese consulate each day, hoping for visas that could allow them to escape the Nazis.

Always the loyal civil servant, Consul-General Chiune Sugihara knew Tokyo would have nothing to do with these Jews; yet, as a Christian, he also knew what would be the right thing to do.

Sugihara cabled Tokyo three times for instructions. When the answer finally came, he was told to refuse anyone who didn't already hold a visa to another country.

But Sugihara knew that none of those at the gates of the consulate had ANYWHERE to go and that no country would accept them, so he made a courageous decision.

For 29 days, around the clock Sugihara kept signing visas…6,000 before he was forced to leave.

Even on the train, he did what he could…handing out blank visas as fast as he could in a desperate attempt to help just one more who would know life because this quiet, dignified Japanese man dared to follow his heart regardless of the cost to himself.

For 29 days, around the clock Sugihara kept signing visas…6,000 before he was forced to leave.

Corrie and Betsie ten Boom

Corrie and Betsie ten Boom and their aging father Casper were moved by their Christian compassion when they saw what was happening to the Jewish families around them in Haarlem. But what could two spinster women and an old man do?

The answer came knocking at their door. It was a Jewish neighbor desperate to find someplace to hide.

With a safe room built into Corrie's bedroom, they began opening their home to any Jew who sought their help.

For the ten Booms, they were only doing what ANY Christian should, but to others, they were traitors.

When the Gestapo arrested them, they offered to release Casper if he'd stop hiding Jews. The old man, his eyes ablaze with the fire of faith, told the officer, "Sir, If I go home today, tomorrow I'll open my door to anyone who knocks for help. I would consider it an honor to give my life for God's Chosen People." A few days later, Casper ten Boom died in prison.

Corrie and Betsie were shipped to the dreaded Ravensbrück Concentration Camp, where Betsie died.

Corrie survived. She spent the rest of her life telling her story of love triumphing over hate in a world of darkness…

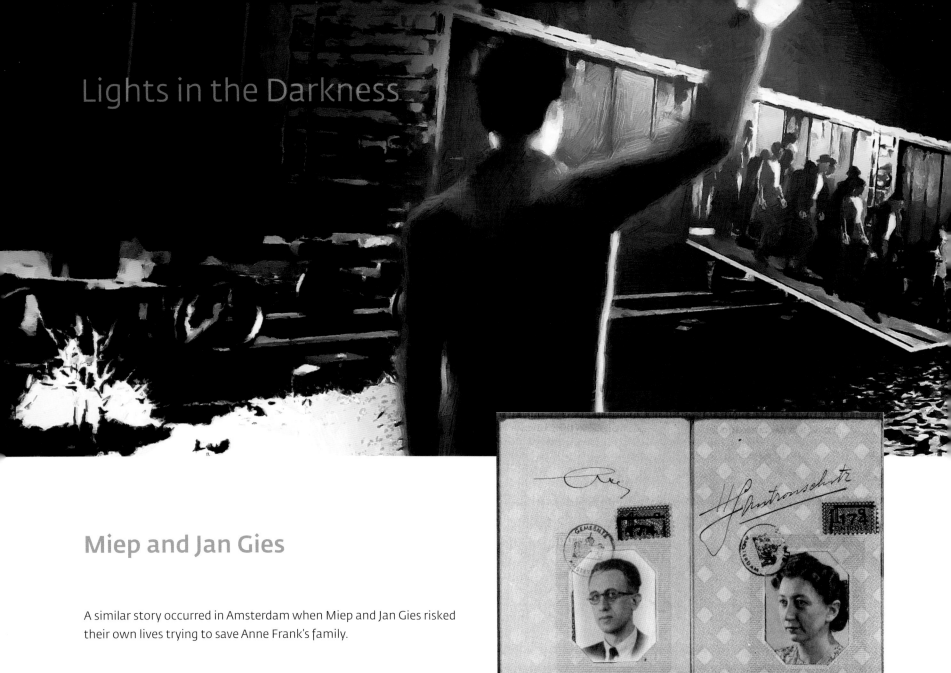

Lights in the Darkness

Miep and Jan Gies

A similar story occurred in Amsterdam when Miep and Jan Gies risked their own lives trying to save Anne Frank's family.

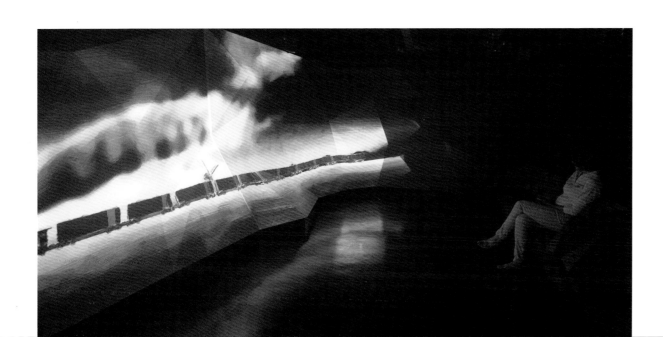

Raoul Wallenberg

In Hungary, 400,000 jews had already been shipped in boxcars to the death camp of Auschwitz. Despite all the dangers, Raoul Wallenberg risked his life and volunteered to go to Hungary as a diplomat for Sweden.

In the dead of winter, Wallenberg joined the thousands of Jewish prisoners in the death marches to Auchwitz, trying to save anyone he could.

He harbored tens of thousands of Jews in buildings he bought as Swedish diplomatic property.

The Nazis couldn't touch them; they were on Swedish sovereign soil – or so he convinced the Nazis!

Lights in the Darkness

The people who walked in darkness Have seen a great light; Those who dwelt in the land of the shadow of death, Upon them a light has shined.

– Isaiah 9:2

One day he jumped onto a train bound for Auschwitz, handing out as many passports to as many people as he could reach...then demanded the Nazi guards release his citizens.

He even convinced the Germans not to blow up the Budapest Ghetto and murder the thousands of innocent lives still trapped inside.

Raoul Wallenberg saved more than 100,000 Jews. He said, "I could never return to Stockholm knowing I had not done everything possible to save the Jews."

Inside the museum gallery are beams of light. Within each one is the name of a person whose life was saved by the conviction of these

Lights in the Darkness...

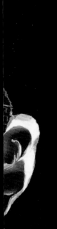

Canada

U.S.A

Belgium

The Brave

The Brave

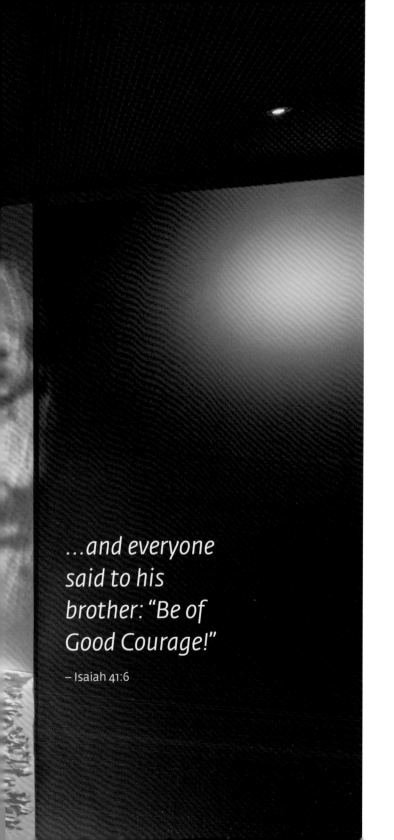

...and everyone said to his brother: "Be of Good Courage!"

– Isaiah 41:6

Here's to the Brave—

Those who fought alongside the Jewish people to establish and defend the state of Israel.

General Marie-Pierre Koenig
Commander of the French Forces of the Interior

We're here in Libya, North Africa.

We have been given the job of holding the allied line here while our British boys have retreated from the field to regroup.

We've held off five German divisions.

Yesterday, just after the British commander sent word they have been off the field, this ragtag company of soldiers stumbled into camp.

Wouldn't you know!?

They were all Jews—part of a unit of British Palestinians called The Jewish Brigade.

Their leader, a Major Liebmann from Tel Aviv, told us his men had been assigned to secure the far end of the French line covering the British army's retreat.

Over 300 of his men had been killed in the fighting, but they had held the line...incredible!

I saw them putting away their flag, a blue Star of David on a white background. They said the British wouldn't let them fly it in their presence. I told them to mount it on my command jeep and gave orders to my officers to salute the new flag of the state of Israel. Of course, it wasn't a nation yet, but I knew it would be! Major Liebmann told me it was the first time anyone outside of their own company ever saluted the Jewish flag.

> Those brave Jewish lads helped us in the face of an overwhelming adversary.

Hats off to those boys. Bravo! They are the real heroes, and they have my friendship for life!

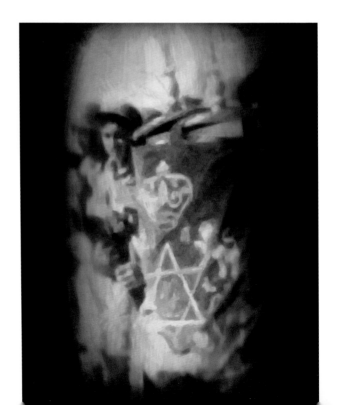

The Brave

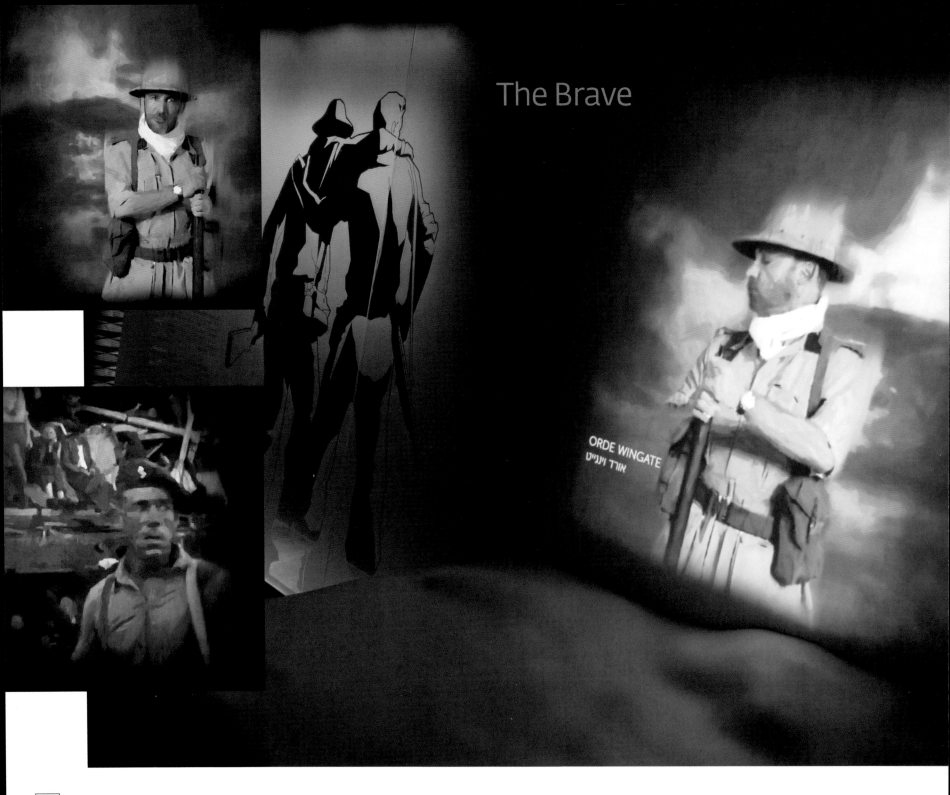

The Brave

ORDE WINGATE
אורד וינגייט

Major Orde Wingate
British Intelligence

They say I was something of a rebel in the British army.

In '36, I was posted to Palestine, British mandate.

Back in 1917 , the original plan was to help the Jews build their homeland—at least that's what a lot of people thought.

Jewish pioneers were coming from everywhere and settling with farms and orchards and towns on the land of their Biblical ancestors. It was like the Bible said, the children of Abraham were coming home. Marvelous…simply marvelous!

At first, we encouraged the idea of all this, even helped it along.

But the government was using their "best endeavors" to BLOCK Jews coming to Palestine—totally on the side of the Arabs who didn't want ANY Jews there.

To make matters worse, every night, local Arabs would band together and raid the Jewish villages, stealing, burning, doing terrible things. I refused to sit by and do nothing!

I knew the way to end this was for the Jews to take the initiative…take the fight to the Arabs instead of waiting to be attacked every night. I went to them and told them they HAD to fight! I mean, really FIGHT! "And you will not win…unless I teach you how to fight, and I lead you into battle."

I trained them how to be guerilla fighters—how to take the fight to the enemy instead of waiting for the enemy to fight you. But I did more than teach them. I led them, showing them by my example that GOOD officers LEAD their men in battle—put themselves out front.

Well, we put a stop to those Arab raids, at least for the time being! It didn't go so well for me, however. The British Army didn't appreciate one of their own acting on his Christian faith and helping the Jews!

In '39, they got their way. I was reassigned to London.

But then, one of the young men I trained was a real fighter named Moshe Dayan.

He went on to become Israel's greatest general. According to Moshe, I taught them "everything they knew."

Not a bad legacy.

To this day, I'm told, if you ask anyone in Israel about Orde Wingate, most often you'll hear them say, "You mean Our Friend?"

At the end of the day, that's the best legacy of all, for any of us. Wouldn't you say?

Harry S Truman
33rd President of the United States

I got the job when the boss, President Roosevelt, up and died on us. I was Vice President, so here we are!

I can think of a lot of reasons why I SHOULDN'T have this job, but Israel isn't one of them.

As a matter of fact, not a year after Israel got their statehood, the Chief Rabbi of Israel...what's his name..Yitzhak Herzog, hell of a nice man...he came to see me. "Mr. President," he says, "God put you in your mother's womb so you would be the instrument to bring about the rebirth of Israel after 2,000 years." Imagine that! Me...'God's instrument.' I have to tell you, I cried. I really did. What did I do?

A lot less than I wanted to do. When I heard what that god-forsaken Hitler was doing to the poor Jews in Europe, I begged the Brits to let more Jews into Palestine. You think they listened? We could've saved a lot of more lives if they'd just let them through.

Of course, it didn't go any easier with our own people. When the United Nations voted to partition Palestine, I stood with the Jews. Took a lot of heat for it. State Department told me if we didn't disavow the vote, we'd lose Arab oil. I said, "The hell with Arab oil!" I told the Secretary of State, "I'll handle this problem not by the light of OIL, but by the light of JUSTICE!"

Now, if I did anything to earn the rabbi's commendation, it was what happened after Mr. Ben-Gurion declared statehood.

Everybody and his brother told me to keep quiet. But I'm from Missouri, and we speak our mind when it counts. Not twelve minutes after Mr. Ben-Gurion finished his speech, I sent a cable, congratulating him and welcoming Israel to the family of nations.

> I had faith in Israel before it was established, I have faith in it now…not just another sovereign nation, but as an embodiment of the great ideals of our civilization.

Well, that's all I have to say about that!

The Brave

The Brave

JOHN PATTERSON

British Army Officer **John Patterson**

Hello there! This rifle made me famous, they tell me. Used it to bag two man-eating lions in Kenya awhile back. Made a lot of news back in London!

But most people don't know what I did in my career that meant the most to me.

At the begining of the Great War, I believe you now call it World War I, hundreds of Jews from British Palestine volunteered to serve...not that anyone at Whitehall was ASKING them to. They did it out of a sense of patriotism. Frankly, the army didn't want the Jews! But the army did need support units, so they formed the Zion Mule Corps and put me in charge. These were brave lads.

I pushed every way I could to get them on the front line where they belonged...where they wanted to be. If the war hadn't dragged on for so long and so many British lads gotten killed, the boys from Palestine might have never had a chance to show their stuff. But the army needed soldiers, so they turned my Mule Corps into a full fighting unit. This was the first Jewish military fighting unit in 2,000 years...led by a Christian...imagine that!

Imagine, too, the surprise in London when my boys started winning battles and proving themselves heroes on the battlefield.

When World War II came along, more than 5,000 young men signed up to serve under the Star of David flag.

That's when I became good friends of Benzion and Tzila Netanyahu. They asked me to be godfather to their son, Yonatan...they even named him after me. His younger brother Benjamin was a sharp one. Of course, no one knew then that Yonatan would be killed rescuing passengers in a terrorist hijacking or that Benjamin would be prime minister someday.

Looking back, I don't believe what I did for Israel was that great, but some believed that if it hadn't been for me, there would be no Jewish state. I doubt that. Still, it's nice to be so remembered by such good friends!

The Promise

saying: "Whom shall I send, And who will go for Us?" Then I said, "Here am I! Send me." – Isaiah 6:8

What does it mean to say "Here am I"?

The Promise

ABRAHAM
Promise that seems Impossible

For Abraham...

it was to receive a promise that seemed impossible...

Now the Lord had said to Abram: "Get out of your country, From your family And from your father's house, To a land that I will show you. I will make you a great nation; I will bless you And make your name great; And you shall be a blessing. I will bless those who bless you, And I will curse him who curses you; And in you all the families of the earth shall be blessed."

—Genesis 12:1-3

JACOB
Trusting in a God

To Isaac...

it meant following a journey to the unknown...

To Jacob...

... trusting in a "God who would prevail"

The Promise

Therefore say to the children of Israel: "I am the Lord; I will bring you out from under the burdens of the Egyptians, I will rescue you from their bondage, and I will redeem you with an outstretched arm and with great judgments. I will take you as My people, and I will be your God. Then you shall know that I am the Lord your God who brings you out from under the burdens of the Egyptians. And I will bring you into the land which I swore to give to Abraham, Isaac, and Jacob; and I will give it to you as a heritage: I am the Lord." —Exodus 6:6-8

MOSES
Voice to Freedom

For Moses...

A call to identify with slaves...

Becoming their voice to freedom...

The Promise

DAVID
Knowing Who Was on HIS side

SOLOMON
Temple to God

I come to you in the name of the Lord of hosts, the God of the armies of Israel, whom you have defied. This day the Lord will deliver you into my hand.
—1 Samuel 17:45-46

David...

Facing a giant...

Knowing Who was on HIS side...

For Solomon...

Building a temple to God...

Thus says the Lord God: "When I have gathered the house of Israel from the peoples among whom they are scattered, and am hallowed in them in the sight of the Gentiles, then they will dwell in their own land which I gave to My servant Jacob. And they will dwell safely there, build houses, and plant vineyards; yes, they will dwell securely, when I execute judgments on all those around them who despise them. Then they shall know that I am the Lord their God." —Ezekiel 28:25-26

EZEKIEL
What CAN be

For Ezekiel...

Understanding that what appears to be does not control what CAN be...

The Promise

Each was given an opportunity...
A moment of decision...

They said "Yes."

For dreamers like Professor George Bush, John Henry Dunant, William Blackstone, and Willem ten Boom...
a call to believe ancient prophecies...a call to service...

And what of the Visionaries?

Edward Robinson	Anthony Ashley Cooper
Laurence and Alice Oliphant	Horatio & Anna Spafford
William Hechler	Josiah Wedgwood
Arthur James Balfour	David Lloyd George
Walter Lowdermilk	Winston Churchill
Woodrow Wilson	Queen Victoria

WILLIAM HECHLER

WALTER LOWDERMILK

WOODROW WILSON

QUEEN VICTORIA

DAVID LLOYD GEORGE

ARTHUR JAMES BALFOUR

WINSTON CHURCHILL

JOSIAH WEDGWOOD

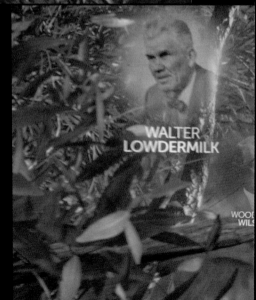

WALTER LOWDERMILK

WOODROW WILSON

VICTORIA

WINSTON
CHURCHILL

and will not forsake My people Israel

—1 Kings 6:12-13

The Promise

OSKAR SCHINDLER

CORRIE BETSIE AND CASPER
TEN BOOM

For many, their choice came at great cost...

Some surrendered complacency to get involved...
OSKAR SCHINDLER

Some took action when others cowered in fear...
CASPER, BETSIE, AND CORRIE TEN BOOM

Others gave up their careers...died poor and forgotten...
CHIUNE SUGIHARA, RAOUL WALLENBERG

They risked their very lives...
IRENA SENDLER

CHIUNE
SUGIHARA

RAOUL
WALLENBERG

IRENA
SENDLER

The Promise

For some it was doing their duty...

But more...a conviction of the heart...

Orde Wingate
Harry Truman
John Patterson
Marie-Pierre Koenig

These heroes of Zionism are but a glimpse of a great mosaic...

Defenders of the Promise...
Friends of the People of Israel...
Custodians of the Covenant...

Each one said "Here Am I" when their call came...

The Promise

Someday...somewhere...

At a moment in your life...

You may have such a call...

An opportunity to pass the torch of this promise forward...

Your decision could determine the future of the Promise of Israel...

What will you do?

Will you say "Here Am I"... as these have done?

If you say "yes" in your moment of decision,

you will become part of this mosaic of the Promise kept...

to be passed to the future...

to generations who have yet to know this Miracle in the Desert.

The Promise

These were the visions of my head while on my bed: I was looking, and behold, A tree in the midst of the earth, And its height was great. The tree grew and became strong; Its

height reached to the heavens, And it could be seen to the ends of all the earth. Its leaves were lovely, Its fruit abundant, And in it was food for all. —Daniel 4:10-12

The Promise

Lift your eyes now and look from the place where you are—northward, southward, eastward, and westward; for all the land which you see I give to you and your descendants...

FOREVER.

—Genesis 13:14-15

About Us

Located in the heart of Jerusalem, the Friends of Zion Museum brings stories of Christian love and heroism to the world. Magnificently told using ground-breaking technology found nowhere else in the nation, visitors experience the unfolding story as though stepping back in time. Accompanied by a moving original musical score, fantastic surround sound, lighting second-to-none, and interactive displays that appear to come to life before your very eyes, the Friends of Zion Museum is a once-in-a-lifetime experience for audiences from around the world. Visitors enter a whole new world where they meet the biblical figures, academics, businessmen, and military officials who, through their faith, have forged an everlasting bond between the Jewish and Christian peoples.